IMAGES
of England

AROUND

WALLASEY

AND

NEW BRIGHTON

On 11 July 1957 HM the Queen is welcomed to Wallasey, as part of her tour of Cheshire, by the Town Clerk, Arthur Harrison, at Wallasey Grove Road station. The Mayor, Ald. Henry Bedlington is looking on.

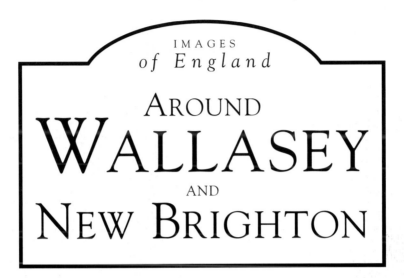

IMAGES
of England

AROUND
WALLASEY
AND
NEW BRIGHTON

Compiled by
Ralph Rimmer

TEMPUS

First published 1996, reprinted 1999, 2001
Copyright © Ralph Rimmer, 1996

Tempus Publishing Limited
The Mill, Brimscombe Port, Stroud,
Gloucestershire GL5 2QG

ISBN 0 7524 0156 4

Typesetting and origination by
Tempus Publishing Limited
Printed in Great Britain by
Midway Colour Print, Wiltshire

This book is dedicated to
Mair and her boys, Trevor, David, Peter, John and Andrew.

In 1978 children from Marymount School planted a tree in the grounds of the school assisted by Lynda Chalker (Lady), Wallasey MP and Minister of Transport. The children later planted trees in a local park.

Contents

His Worshipful the Mayor of Wirral, Councillor Walter Smith, and the Mayoress, his wife, Betty.

As a youngster the Mayor was a member of the Boys' Brigade. He is immediately behind the drummer on the left hand side of the picture.

INTRODUCTION

By

THE WORSHIPFUL THE MAYOR OF WIRRAL
(COUNCILLOR WALTER SMITH)

I am delighted to make a contribution to this publication. Photographs
are a pleasant reminder of our past and arouse nostalgia in all of us.

Many people have visited Wallasey by Ferry Boat to enjoy a walk along
our magnificent promenades and sample the leisure facilities. Many
of us who came as visitors (I lived in Liverpool) ended up as
residents, in my family's case as a result of the Second World War
bombing of our Liverpool home.

I enjoyed my upbringing in Wallasey, the area was so different to my
life in Liverpool. There were Summer days spent at the Derby Bathing
Pool (the residents' pool), swimming, diving, sunning ourselves and
running round the pool in a sort of mini-marathon race. The Bidston
Marshes were close by for fishing and raft building, they also gave
us an opportunity to study plants, birds and newts – it was a marvellous
nature study area. Alas the area has been destroyed by motorway and
industrial building development.

When I became a teenager I sought a different social life – dancing on
the New Brighton Pier to the Eddie Mendoza Seven or a Saturday night
at the Tower Ballroom.

I attended Oxton Road Methodist Church and was a member of the Youth
Club where I met my wife, Betty, and made many friends there.
After our wedding we came to live in Birkenhead where we reside happily
but I will always think myself lucky to have been brought up in Wallasey.

As the Mayor of Wirral I was pleased to be asked by my friend, Ralph,
for this contribution.

With Best Wishes.

Walter W. Smith

MAYOR

Mayor's Parlour,
Town Hall,
Wallasey,
Wirral,
L44 8ED

February 1996.

The Recorders of Wallasey

Dr Johnson had his Boswell to record his life. Wallasey is particularly well served by recorders of its life. The following have been welcome sources of information and inspiration: J. Appleton; Carol Bidston (author); F. Biddle; A. Fellowes (Moreton); Kenneth Burnley (author); Ian and Marolyn Boumphrey (*Yesterday's Wirral*); Clive Garner (co-author *Silver Screens of Wirral*); T.B. Maund (transport); J. Ryan (railways), Oxton Studios and others. Wirral Libraries have assisted in the provision of photographs through its chief librarian, J.C.W. Norton Esq. Special help, knowledgeable guidance and information have been readily given by Mrs Jenny Done and Mrs Teresa Ashton in the Local History section of Wallasey Central Library. Noel Smith and Joy Hockey helped with corrections to the 2001 reprint.

A special debt is owed to the following recorders who have loaned photographs and shared their unique information to help to make a chronicle of the latter years of the first Milennium upon which their work and this book is based.

Joy Hockey (*née* Rutherford) B.Arch.(Hons) ARIBA is an indefatigable historian of Wallasey. She believes in sharing her knowledge. She taught local history at Wallasey FE College and had a weekly column on local history in the Wallasey News. She is married to Philip Hockey a retired river pilot who has been a lifeboatman for over forty years. They are both keen sailors and members of the Wallasey Yacht Club. Joy is the Chairman of Wallasey Historical Society and a member of the Wallasey Civic Society.

Noël Smith is an unceasing seeker after the history of Wallasey and especially of its residents. Like Joy Hockey, Noël also believes in disseminating the information he gleans. He has published two books, *Almost an Island* (1981), reprinted several times, and *Sandstone and Mortar* (1991). The former deals with the intimate history of Wallasey and is illustrated with interesting anecdotes while the latter is more concerned with the people of Wallasey and their contributions to its life. They are a fine source of local history. Noël lives with his wife, Eva, in Rake Lane.

The photographic career of Ron Smith, Noël's brother, can be followed by the cameras he used. He began with a box camera converted to take 35 mm film before investing in a Woolworth's bakelite camera, a VP Twin. He graduated to an Agfa Karat and when he became a semi-professional he used Exacta and Speed Graphic cameras. As a professional associate of Medley and Bird and as a freelance he used Nikon, Rolleiflex and Hasselblad cameras. Irrespective of the cameras he used, he was the skilled and polished professional behind them.

Keith Medley served his apprenticeship with Durando Mills of Lime Street, Liverpool, and worked for Jerome's of London Road who provided three portraits for half-a-crown (12p). He graduated to working for Lintas, Blackfriars, London, specialising in industrial and advertising photography. Keith was responsible for the pre-war Lever Bros. 'girls in bubble baths' advertisements. After work with the internationally renowned portrait photographer, Howard Coster, Keith joined a RAF experimental unit where he met Bob Bird. They began a business in Wallasey by taking 'Walkie' photographs on the promenade and developed a complete photographic service until the partners went their separate ways into still, movie and television photojournalism.

Bob Bird's experience as a beach photographer at Margate and Folkestone gained him a post as photographer at the Air Ministry. When war arrived he became a civilian airborne photographer, serving at Beaulieu, Hants., and at Helensborough on the Clyde. When the firm of Medley and Bird developed after the war, Keith Medley, Bob Bird and their staff must have photographed every group and every public event in Wallasey. Robin Bird brought out *A Bird's Eye View of Merseyside*, a golden treasury of press photographs from 1949 to 1999, in his memory.

One

Around Moreton and Leasowe

Mary Anne is symbolic of Moreton's rural past as she stands outside her farmhouse in about 1910. Dore Farm and Dore Cottage are to the rear. She appeared on Moreton souvenirs and is remembered in the naming of Old Marylands Lane. Although by derivation Moreton was a hamlet by the mere and part of the manor of Bidston, its inhabitants were the largest taxpayers in Wirral. In 1801 it had twice the population of Birkenhead. By 1949 its 1000th post-war house had been opened and the township is flourishing with its 25,000 residents. It has now become a commonplace for shoppers to come to Moreton as it used to be for busloads from Moreton to go to Birkenhead and Liscard.

In 1918 a lone carthorse waits outside Moreton Church of England School. With a population of 361 in Moreton in 1860, William Inman, the shipping magnate, headed a subscription list to build a school on land donated by J.R. Shaw Esq. of Arrowe Hall. The school was opened on Thursday 21 February 1861.

In 1903 the children of the school posed outside the building. Within a month of opening in 1861, sixty three children were in attendance under its head teacher, Miss Ruth Dixon (Mrs Sparks), appointed at £31 a year. The heavy footwear of the children was necessary as many children came from farms and most of the local roads were inaccessible. Attendance was often boosted by children holidaying at the Leasowe camp site. The old school was demolished in 1973.

In 1961 Moreton Church of England School, now in Upton Road, celebrated its centenary with an exhibition. On Saturday 8 April 1961 the Mayor and Mayoress of Wallasey, Ald. C.G.E. Dingle and Mrs Dingle, attended the exhibition. Mr John Appleyard is on the extreme left. He was the first headmaster to have been appointed. He succeeeded Miss Irving and Miss Bellis, who had been the head for twenty-four years. Also on the left of the picture are Mrs Irving and Mr Irving, the Borough Librarian, who designed the exhibition. The children in the front are Paul Appleyard (10), Robert Slee (9), Stephen Fox (10) and Janice Barkley (10).

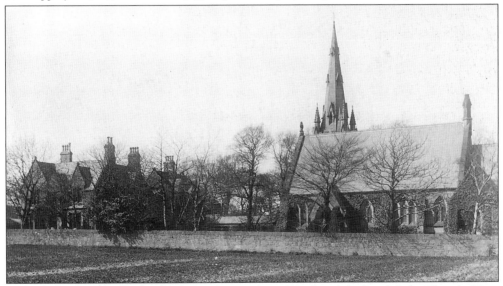

In 1910 Christ Church still had its rectory next door. The church had replaced a Chapel of Rest pulled down in about 1690 which probably stood near to the present post office. William Inman, shipping magnate of Upton Hall,who pioneered the use of screw driven vessels and carried mails to America, was the main benefactor in the building of the church. Local landowner, Thomas Webster, gave the land. Its first minister, the Revd M. Fearnley, was inducted on Thursday 30 July 1863. Today the church is enhanced by its community centre and its broad commitment to people of the locality.

MORETON VILLAGE.

This postcard, showing a group of three men outside the Plough Inn, was posted in 1924. From the eighteenth century the Plough had been used as a refreshment stop for the gentry on their way from Chester to the Leasowe races. 'Dags' Davies was its notable landlord during the Second World War. The plantation on the left was used as a pinfold for securing stray animals. The trees were taken down in 1926. The Rimmer family had a smithy nearby.

MORETON CROSS, MORETON.

In the 1930s, as the bus approaches the Plough, two young ladies cross in Birkenhead Road. Among shopkeepers opposite the plantation who have been remembered are Hetty Dodd, confectioner, Nellie Usher, postmistress, Thomas, grocer and baker, Mrs Rudkin, fish and greengrocery, Bell's, newsagent, and Watling's, post office and chandlery. There was interesting local transport to be seen around the Cross in the 1920s, including a chain driven bus and a charabanc with solid tyres.

In about 1950 the Coach and Horses looks as tranquil as it did in 1933 when it offered threecourse luncheons from 1/6 (7p) and could accommodate large parties up to 200. Before the inn was enlarged the Stone was placed at the corner, known as Carthouse End, to prevent cartwheels damaging the building, was the meeting place of the village. The shop with the awning nearer to the Midland Bank had been Fanny Birch's lending library and sweetshop. It had steps leading down and was subject to flooding.

In about 1924 a milk cart is standing outside Lunt's cake shop in Station Road (now Pasture Road). The Picture House was built on the site of old cottages and the village pump. It was opened on Saturday 30 April 1921. One of its earliest films was *Her Benny*, based on a novel by Silas Hocking with an appropriate Liverpool setting. The cinema closed on 28 March 1964.

Road to Shore, Moreton

In about 1910 a coal cart waits by Sunny Side in Pasture Road. It belonged to George John Spredbury who was the chief cashier of the Mobil Oil Co. at the Penny Bridge. He ran the coal company as a sideline. His granddaughter, Barbara (Mrs Stan Ellison) still lives in Moreton.

In 1962 employees of the British Railways plant, on a works outing, look at the manufacture of chocolates at the Cadbury factory. Land was drained near the fence, seen in the previous picture, to build the chocolates and chocolate biscuits factory in 1953. Following the 1960s Cadbury-Schweppes merger it became part of the Premier Brands Group, which included Typhoo Tea.

In 1927 there is a flood outside the home of F. 'Tich' Mason near the Birket Bridge and Pasture Farm in Pasture Road (looking towards the shore). 'Tich' Mason, champion jockey six times between 1901 and 1907, won the 1905 Grand National on Kirkland. This was the name which he gave to the bungalow he had built on the opposite side of the road, now occupied by Kirkland Kennels. The shops on the right hand side were pulled down in the 1930s.

In about 1925 the dwellers in low-lying areas like Kerrs Field, off Pasture Road, were subjected to frequent flooding. They lived happily enough in makeshift homes, including former holiday bungalows, old railway carriages and old buses, enjoying the freedom from paying rates. It was said that they used punts to go shopping in Moreton. They certainly had to paddle through flood water and carry towels to dry their feet. The dwellings were cleared away between 1928 and 1939.

Leasowe Lighthouse was built in 1824 although a date stone over the door, 1763, refers to an earlier building. The Williams family from Llandudno were appointed as keepers and when Mr Williams died in 1892, Mrs Williams became the first woman lighthouse keeper in the country. She later used the building as a café. The Williams family from left to right was: Bertha, Rose, Mrs Williams, Aggie, Eva and, seated front, Dolly. Mrs Williams died in 1935.

After the First World War camping on Leasowe Common grew as an economical holiday venue because of the reputation of the quality of air at Moreton shore. The Leasowe Camping Association held an annual gala there. George Henry Lee, high class Liverpool department store, sent its employees for weekend camping; men one week and women the next.

On 20 July 1962 the first Hovercraft regular passenger service in the world was inaugurated by British United Airways/Vickers Armstrong at the Moreton/Leasowe shore. When the service began over 3,000 people booked on the twenty-four passenger Vickers VA3 for the nineteen minutes, twenty-four miles, service from Wallasey to Rhyl at £1 single or £2 return. (Photo: K. Medley)

Each passenger on the service was given a ticket/ picture postcard/ souvenir all-in-one. A first day commemoration franking was available and mail was carried on the Hovercraft.

In 1904 Leasowe Castle became a hotel and hydropathic establishment and here residents are taking tea in about 1905. It was built as an octagonal tower for housing hawks and horses and as a viewpoint for watching the Leasowe Races which were held in May between 1672 and 1723. They were the forerunner of the Wallasey Stakes at Newmarket. The first St Bernard dog in Britain was brought to the castle by a Waterloo veteran.

Here is the entrance hall of Leasowe Castle after 1910 when it was purchased for use as a Railway Convalescent Home. The wrought iron rails of the banister of the Battle Staircase numbered eighty four and fittings in the library were made from wood from the local submerged forest. By 1971 it housed only a few carers and cleaners but in 1980 became a hotel again. The first Wallasey semi-public horsedrawn transport took visitors between the Castle and Seacombe Ferry.

This is the New Brighton RUFC on 2 May 1962 which had become the leading club in the country, securing 548 to 227 points. Left to right in the picture are, front: Tomkins, Jordan. Seated: Mustard, Ridge, Hart, Wright, Staniford, Cooper. Back: Taylor, Lander, Flood, Bullivant; Wynne Thomas, Owen; Ibison, Townsend, Gibson. The club was established in 1875 and after playing at Rake Lane, Seabank Road and Seaview Road has settled in Reeds Lane, Leasowe. F.P. Jones played for England in 1893 and V.R. Tindall gained four English caps in 1951.

It was possible to follow more leisurely pursuits in the 'Bungalow Town', between Leasowe Road and the shore, which was popular in the 1920s and 1930s especially. Even local Wallaseyans would spend holidays there. Once over the dunes the refreshing air from the Irish Sea was waiting. Here in this 1933 picture are Mrs Addyman and her daughter Mrs Jones from Childer Thornton with their visitors, Joe and Eva Rimmer, future Mayor and Mayoress of Ellesmere Port, and a seven year old Ralph Rimmer.

By 1900 Leasowe Road bore little resemblance to the original meandering muddy lane. As roads improved cycling became popular. In 1889 Dunlop introduced pneumatic tyres although cyclists were dubious about them. In 1894 free wheels and in 1899 variable gears were refinements. This lady's cycle has a chain guard to prevent her long dress becoming entangled as she rides away from Wallasey.

Looking from the Wallasey Village end of Leasowe Road in about 1912, it is possible to see that the railway bridge now indicates that there is a station adjacent. Leasowe Road, Wallasey Village, station was opened in 1907. Many of the houses in Leasowe Road were occupied by market gardeners whose land was nearby. Wallasey potatoes and tomatoes were even recognised by gourmets in London.

On 7 November 1967 HRH the Duchess of Kent arrived at Birket Avenue in Leasowe to open the new Wallasey Grammar School for boys. She was accompanied by Lord Leverhulme, the Lord Lieutenant of Cheshire, and S. Harvey, the Deputy Chief Constable of Cheshire. Rex Bird, a school prefect, carries a protective umbrella. This was the sixth building to house the school. (Photo: R. Smith)

In March 1995 HRH the Duchess of Kent revisited the Wallasey School, now a comprehensive mixed school as part of the quadricentenary celebrations.The Duchess of Kent is being presented with a bouquet, watched by pupils of the school and, from left to right: Peter Johnson, master at the school, the Revd Richard Orton, Rector of St Hilary's and Chairman of the Governors, and the Lord Lieutenant and his wife.

On Speech Day in December 1962 the Deputy Head Boy of Wallasey Grammar School, D.W.M. Bygroves, presents a book to the speaker Lord Justice Sellars. Also in the picture from left to right are Ernest Marples, (Minister of Transport) H.J. Oliver (Head Master), R.S. Gandy (Head boy), Ald. C.G.E. Dingle, Lady Sellars and the Mayor of Wallasey, Ald. E. Glyn Roberts

More than thirty years later at the Wallasey School 1991-1992 Speech Day, Head Boy Andrew Beattie relaxes with the Mayor and Mayoress of Wirral, Cllr. and Mrs Frank Jones.

Two
Around Wallasey Village

'Croeso i'r Ynys!' 'Welcome to the Welshman's Island!' On 11 July 1957 a royal attendant offers an umbrella to HM the Queen at Grove Road Station, Wallasey Village, as she steps out, escorted by the Mayor of Wallasey, Alderman Henry Bedlington. (Photo: Ron Smith)

HARRISON DRIVE, WALLASEY

In the early 1920s a sign on the lamp states that 'All Trams Stop Here' as a lady and two children wait hopefully. Large numbers of people are making their way to the sea at Harrison Drive. Even at Grove Road, a small station opened in 1888, the Station Master had a set of livery which was worn for the arrival of special visitors. The Station Master's house, in the foreground on the left, still stands but the front garden disappeared when the road was widened.

GROVE ROAD, WALLASEY

Although this postcard was sent in 1924, the presence of the Tower in the background suggests that the picture was taken before 1919 when the demolition of the Tower began. The tram moving along Grove Road is destined for Poulton as the 'P' on the front of the tram indicates.

In 1945 young members of the Women's League of Health and Beauty line up by the grounds of the Grange, Grove Road. It had been built as the home of Major W. Chambres who had previously lived in Mosslands. On 5 April 1924 the Grange was opened as a park.

Here is a group of adult members of the League of Health and Beauty on 30 April 1962. The movement was founded in 1930 by Mary Bagot Stack for the enjoyment of exercise and movement to music to improve posture and flexibility. One Wallasey branch was formed in 1933, meeting in the Memorial Hall, Manor Road, Somervile School Hall and Oldershaw School. The branch closed in 1985. Other former members remember meeting in Emmanuel Church Hall and St Luke's Church Hall. Mavis Budge is recalled as one of the teachers in the local movement. In 1995 the League held its 65th birthday in the Albert Hall.

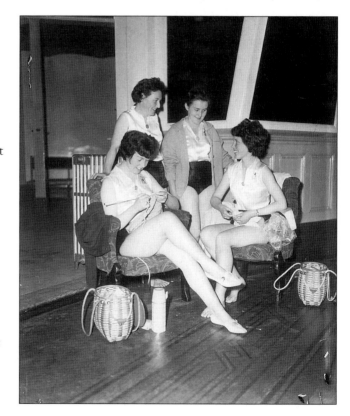

In 1912 Doris and Charlie Chaloner enjoy the fresh air outside their family home, 'Sandbrae', Seafield Drive. Doris was well known in sports circles and later became Mrs Doris Redford Davies. Charlie, an accountant, became a governor of Upton Hall School and has remained in the family home all his life.

In about 1936 Ralph Brookes-Ball married Gladys Earley, a physiotherapist and sportswoman. The reception was held at the Grange. Wearing a top hat is John Alfred Earley with Jessica Earley (*née* Bolshaw), and, on the extreme right, Bill Earley, a well known regular at the 'Vic.'

In the 1920s the Grove Temperance Hotel, with ninety rooms and a billiard hall, became a café. Next door to the hotel was the Criterion Bazaar selling souvenirs and novelties. The name 'Criterion' is still retained by the present owner of the confectionery and newspapers business.

On 2 May 1962 Ald. C.G.E. Dingle attended a charity coffee morning at the Melody Inn. The Melody Inn Club was upstairs in the former Grove Court and opened in 1957 offering dancing every night and English, Chinese and Continental meals until midnight. In the 1960s the building was demolished after a fire.

The old Lighthouse Inn, known as the fishermen's inn, was built between 1827 and 1830 next door to the Lighthouse Cottage. There were market gardens opposite. Some of the adjoining buildings were knocked down to construct the more luxurious new inn.

In 1955 Wallasey Village still had Willow Cottage, one of the many cottages that gave the village its character. The plaque on the wall indicates that its first owners 'R.I.O.M.' built the cottage in 1737 and its name was derived from a large willow tree that grew in the garden. Willow Cottage disappeared when both sides of the road from Leasowe Road to Sandy Lane were widened in 1962. It had taken 750 years to end the Wallasey Village bottleneck or to destroy the village charm, according to some residents.

In 1963 J.Hickling took this night shot of the Phoenix for the *Wallasey Grammar School Magazine*. In 1940 the Coliseum in Wallasey Village was bombed and it was not until 1951 when Leslie Blond, proprietor of the Continental Cinema, built the 'Phoenix' in the Coliseum's ashes. It had unique soundproof cry areas where adults could take small children, hear and see the film but not disturb anyone else. The last film shown was in 1983 and sheltered accommodation replaced the demolished building in 1988.

In 1932 Claremount Tennis Club held a party. In the middle of the back row is Renée Earley. Some of the others at the party are Phyllis Earley, Ray Leslie and Mrs Leslie.

Here is the Wallasey Village Festival or 'Club Day' being held in the late 1920s. The parade assembled in St George's School, marched behind the Wallasey Silver Band through the village until it reached a field near the Cottage Hospital in Claremount Road. There were sideshows, coconut shies, slow bicycle races and dancing around a maypole.

In 1929 this float had raised £375 for the Women's Cottage Hospital. The Cottage Hospital was originally in St George's Road (Back Lane) and moved to Claremount Road in 1885, providing treatment for both sexes, males only and finally women only. It was closed in 1980 and Nightingale Lodge is now in its place.

This is a class in St George's Road Council School in 1908. The school for boys was opened on 9 March 1907. St Hilary's parish school for young girls was opened in 1847 and transferred to an extension of St George's Road School in 1907.

This is the champion cricket team of St George's Road School in 1932. The team only lost one of its ten games and scored 651 runs against the opposition's 312. The Head Master, Mr Hill, is on the right. Bill York, son of a Wallasey Village grocer, still has his 1932 school cap. He has identified the teacher on the bottom left as Mr Giles (woodwork) and above him, Mr Webster (senior teacher).

A class in St.George's School in 1952. Among the children here are, from left to right, back row: M. Jackson, M. Lewis, C. Whitehead, G. Chambers, D. Fletcher, R. Peers, T. Triplett, J. Franks, G. Evans, B. Tregilgas or A. Monahan. Third row: P. Hickmott, D. Bowers, P. Skinner, R. Tankard, D. Lovatt, R. Burgess, D. Greetham, G. Lord, J. Plowright, I. Wright, R. Thomas, A. Park. Second row: G. Haslam (standing), V. Little, P. Mann, G. Johns, A. Jackson, V. Waters, J Holtham, P. Rennie, P. Newman, C. Noble, G. Brennan, G. Reed, G. Tickle, F. Hughes, G. Lewis (standing). Front row: P. Rowe, B. Phillips, D. Hignett, V. Bellis, H. Crowther, A. Woods, J. Roberts, I. MacKechnie, H. Atkinson, C. May.

In 1954 pupils in a class of infants in St George's School read their reports on investigative learning.

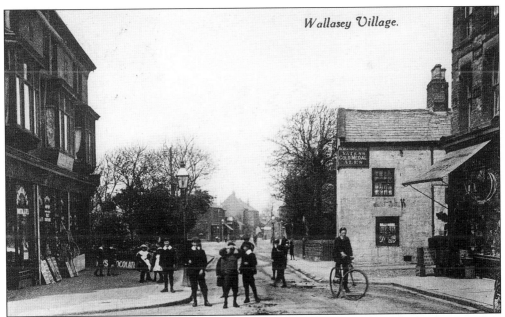

A postcard sent in 1918 shows schoolboys wearing starched collars and knickerbockers standing in the 'bottleneck' by the Black Horse. Originally it was a cottage with a cobbled approach and with a lantern over its door. The inn was built in 1722 and said to be named after a horse owned by Lord Molyneux which he raced at Leasowe. At one time the ale came from Spragg's Brewery in Leasowe Road until taken over by Yates's. The inn was demolished when the road was widened in 1931 and a new Black Horse built nearby.

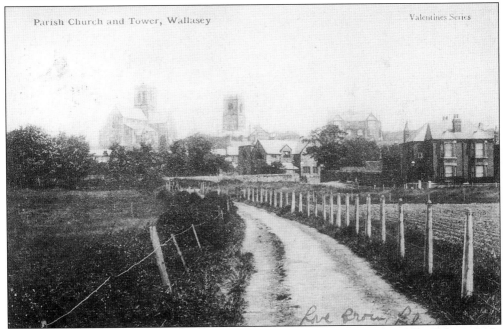

Parish Church and Tower, Wallasey

Valentines Series

In 1905 a walk to St Hilary's church was quite a rural one especially along the Bidston Path. The tower of the old church and the new church are both visible. The new church was built in 1859 from insurance compensation from the fire of 1857 and by public subscription.

In 1903 only the tower remains of the 1530 church which was burnt down in 1857. Probably, there had formerly been two Wallasey churches, Lees Kirk, near Kirkway, and Walleys Kirk in the present churchyard. The church is dedicated to St Hilary of Poitiers, a male with Irish Celtic connections, who died in AD 366. He gained notoriety as the first composer of hymns which he wrote to counteract the propaganda of the secular songs of the heretic Arius. The hymns were too theological to gain popularity.

Here is a look inside St Hilary's church in about 1905. In recent years the pews have been replaced by chairs. Stained glass windows were damaged during the 1940-41 blitz. In 1955 a new east window was made at the Whitefriars Glass Studios, Middlesex, and installed.

OLD CHURCH WALLASEY 1850.

This artist's impression of St Hilary's church in 1850 also shows Wallasey Hall, the home of the Meoles family. The small part sticking out was the Grammar School which had been built in 1799. Wallasey Mill, built from the local sandstone in 1765, is seen in the rear on the high ground of the Breck.

View from the Breck, Wallasey

This view from the Breck in about 1910 shows, on the right, the dwelling converted from the old school house. A new school was built in Back Lane (St George's Road) in 1864 and each desk was equipped with a candle and a holder for dark days. Growing numbers of boys in the school necessitated a move to Withens Lane in 1876. The white building was 'Hillside' where lived a Miss Rimmer, daughter of an artist and photographer. Hillside Road now crosses the site.

Bit of Old Wallasey.

In about 1910 four ladies, a boy and a baby pose for a photograph in Folly Gut off Folly Lane (now part of the Broadway). It was a short cut to St Hilary's church and graveyard.

Photographed about 1905, on the left is Carlile's Cottage, belonging to Henry Carlile, a market gardener, and on the right is Salisbury Cottage, belonging to Sam Salisbury, a Wallasey greengrocer. These were among the last surviving thatched cottages. A wartime bomb accounted for one and road widening for the other.

This scene of Wallasey Village and School Lane (on the right) in about 1900 shows a semi-timbered thatched cottage used as a general shop by Mr Jones. It was pulled down in 1921. The Ring o' Bells Inn is on the right side of the picture and the Old Cheshire Cheese was around the corner on the left. The large house on St Hilary's Brow, seen above the shop in the picture, was called 'Wyncliffe'.

This scene of the Breck was taken some time after 1906 for the Philco Co. of London (fl.1906-1934). The Breck was bought in 1845 by Sir John Tobin for quarrying. He also ran the community flour mill where flour could be bought direct. Millthwaite, the large house in the picture, was built in 1887 and the mill was taken down. Its first owner, George Hunter Peers (1846-1914), Chairman of the Wallasey Board, set up a temperance club for the men of the village.

Breck Road, Wallasey.

In about 1904 School Lane is on the right in this picture of St Hilary's Brow. There is a huddle of four people whom the writer of a postcard recognised as, herself (Katie), her father and Rita and Roy outside their house.

In the 1920s a girl looks down from Breck Road over the one and half mile footpath to Bidston. The upper part of Wallasey Pool is just visible in the distance. The house on the left is 'Mosslands' after which Mosslands Drive is named. It was the home of Captain Chambres, Commanding Officer, No. 3 Company, the Cheshire Regiment, who later lived in the Grange, Grove Road, from 1880.

Three

Around Poulton and Seacombe

In the 1970s two boys play in the West Float dwarfed by the ships in dock.

This is the Penny Bridge photographed in the late 1890s. The original Halfpenny Bridge was built in 1842 and owned by R.C. de Grey Vyner Esq. It became the first and only means of direct communication with Birkenhead. The 1896 Penny Bridge replaced it. When a new bridge was opened on 19 July 1926 the toll was abolished. The boat house (1892) next to it belonged to the Liverpool Victoria Rowing Club. (Photo: Oxton Studios: 01516528690)

In May 1995 Wallasey School held its Quadricentenary Regatta in the West Float. In the Wallasey boat in the foreground are, left to right: Neil Bascombe, Alastair McNichol, Gary Davenport, Neil Thomas, Nevil Andrews, John Carruthers, Peter Duff.

A class of children at Poulton School in 1928 which includes Douglas Ellison whose brother, Stan, provided the photograph.

In 1948 the first team to play for Poulton School after the Second World War won the Junior Championship, losing only one match during the season. Some of the players recalled by Barrie Dennis (second from right, back row) are, back row: Billy McLachlan, Brian Ravenscroft, Alan Fenner (goalkeeper) and John McLachlan.

There were shops along both sides of Poulton Road owned by people called Lloyd, including a baker and a pawnbroker, so that the part by Wheatland Lane became known as Lloyd's Corner. These houses have been replaced by shops with the fronts brought forward. The Queen's Cinema was on the left and it was opened on 4 November 1911. It was luxurious with crimson plush upholstery and with the Paramount Orchestra to accompany the silent images. It closed in 1959 and has since been used as a car showroom and a supermarket.

In the early 1900s a group of youngsters gather in Sherlock Lane, off Limekiln Lane, Poulton. Poulton was originally a small fishing village with its own station from 1895. Rita Hunter the world renowned opera star was born in the area. It was ahead of the other townships with its industries; a vitriol works, a limekiln and a copper works.

In the late 1970s a No. 10 bus on the New Brighton-Clatterbridge route is seen crossing Duke Street Bridge which linked up with Gorsey Lane, Wallasey and was publicly opened on 9 April 1924. Early morning travellers, in particular, used to have to allow an extra twenty minutes for the journey in case the bridge was up. It was also a useful excuse for tardy risers who arrived late for work!

On 20 June 1959 a large grain warehouse in Wallasey Docks caught fire. Engines from 125 brigades in Lancashire and Cheshire joined in to combat the flames. Over £500,000 worth of damage was caused. The press photographer has been able to isolate one of the firemen against the jets from the firemen in the background. The barge Buckwheat is being used by the firemen in their bid to fight the blaze. (Photo: R. Smith)

This is a reproduction of an 1841 watercolour drawing of the Seacombe Pottery by E. Beattie as featured in Hilda Gamlin's (1897) *Twixt Mersey and Dee*. It was near to today's Kelvin Road area. John Goodwin opened his pottery in 1852 and continued there until 1856. He died the following year and was buried in St John's churchyard. His son, Thomas Orton Goodwin, continued the business until 1864. Much of the pottery was shipped abroad and, it is said, a cargo ship disaster carrying uninsured goods from the pottery eventually caused the business to fail.

When Goodwin moved from the Potteries to Seacombe he brought 115 workers with him, including women and children. He provided houses for them. Here is one in Wheatland Lane photographed in 1980.

A train waits in the station at Seacombe in the 1930s. The Seacombe branch line, with a first stop at Liscard and Poulton by Mill Lane, was opened on 1 January 1895. From 1898 trains ran from Seacombe to Hawarden. Before the line opened local residents were entirely dependent on ferries to travel anywhere.

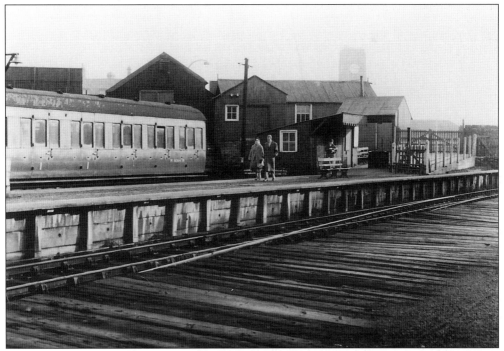

The station was still being used in the 1950s and the picturesque scenery of the Seacombe to Wrexham line was preferred by many to the Birkenhead to Wrexham via Chester route. Many Sunday school excursions to Caergwrle Castle and other North Wales picnic areas began here.

It is 1959 and a car waits outside Seacombe Station, which from its inception had always had a temporary appearance. On 3 January 1960 the Seacombe line was closed to passengers and in 1963 it ceased to carry goods.

Although this is 1903 the layout of the landing stage is very familiar. The gangways are as many remember them and the waiting room is on the right as recalled. In 1797 it cost 2d (c. 1p) for market people and 6d (2p) for the 'Upper Order of People' to cross to Liverpool. In 1861 the Wallasey Local Board took over the running of the ferries from the Coulbourn brothers. In 1915 a twelve months season ticket to Liverpool cost £1 2s 6d (£1.12p) and boats left the ferry every quarter of an hour.

The four storey Seacombe Ferry Hotel, built in 1870 and depicted here in about 1976, had always been regarded as a 'posh' place for the 'toffs'. Formal dress was required for those eating there while listening to its Palm Court orchestra. Before 1890 the shore came up to the embankments and to the doors of the Marine Hotel. The Ferry Hotel had pleasure grounds, a rustic summer houses overlooking the river for the ladies and, for the gentlemen, an American bowling alley. The Ferry Hotel had sadly deteriorated before it closed in 1978.

This was Seacombe Ferry approach in the 1920s. The old clock is still there but was removed in 1930 when the ferry buildings were redesigned. The preponderance of motor cars and the absence of trams suggests that it was a scene during the general strike of 1926. (Photo: Oxton Studios: 01516528690)

The Seacombe Ferry Municipal Garage shown in 1933 was part of the improvements schedule. It was 250 feet long and held 200 cars. It was one of the largest car parks outside London and was approached by a ramp from the ground floor. In 1933 it cost 6d (2p) for 6 hours for cars and 3d (1p) for motor cycles.

Wallasey Corporation shows off its fleet of buses in the 1930s. There are four Leyland Titan TD1, Leyland bodies 1928-29, open staircase buses, and two AEC Regent English Electric, 1935 bodies, buses waiting. Boat passengers in 1933, for instance, used to find buses along twelve routes awaiting their arrival.

The Wallasey Ferry AFC team of 1913-14 played in local Merseyside leagues and a team bearing the name was still active in the 1950s.

Seacombe United AFC the 1908-9 winners of Wirral Intermediate Division won twenty five of their twenty six games, scoring 118 goals to 18 against. Top row, left to right: A. Williams, W. Allandale, J. Roddick, T. Dennis, T. Birks, G. Williams, W. Hitchmough, D. Davies, W. Roddick (trainer). Bottom row: J. Cosgrove (Hon. Sec.), J. Woods, W. Jones, J. Birks (Capt.), D. Green, R. Birkett.

In 1892 Somerville School Primary School was opened in Seacombe. Its first Headmaster was Albert Heap who went on to Gorsedale School and retired in 1938. Joe Lynch, a former pupil received an Albert Medal for saving a fellow crew member from drowning in 1879. The pupils appear very well dressed for an elementary school of the period with their Eton collars and their pocket watches and chains. There was also a private school called 'Somerville' opened just before the First World War on the corner of Albion Street and Victoria Road. Its sports days were held in the Tower grounds.

This is the Irving Theatre in 1906 which had been opened by Sir Henry Irving on 18 December 1899. It began with classical dramas like *Hamlet* and *The Sign of the Cross* but to fill its 2,500 seats comedies like *Charley's Aunt* and artistes like Wee Georgie Wood and Stanley Jefferson (Stan Laurel) became more prevalent. By 1912 it was including films in its programme to the accompaniment of its Philharmonic Orchestra. It went through a number of transformations until, as the Embassy cinema, it closed on 21 March 1959.

A busy scene in Brighton Street, Seacombe, in about 1918, shows a tram travelling via Seaview Road and advertising Owen Owen a Liverpool department store. Note the high wheels on the perambulator in the foreground. The collapsible hood of the pram shows a development from the wicker work or wooden bassinet. In the early 1900s Brighton Street Church provided Christmas lunches for up to 600 needy persons, mostly children.

In the 1920s the lady bowls champion demonstrates her style before fellow members of the Borough Bowling Club which used to play in Demesne Road.

During the construction of the Kingsway Tunnel, 'The Mole', the largest boring machine in the world, began working in 1966 and moved about four feet an hour. It was kept on course by a laser beam. After twenty-seven months it finally emerged in Liverpool on 4 March 1970. (Photo: Medley)

Her Majesty the Queen opens the second tunnel, Kingsway, on 24 June 1971. Others in the photograph are Viscount Leverhulme, the Mayor of Wallasey, Ald H.T.K. Morris, the Town Clerk, Mr A.G. Harrison, and Mrs Harrison. (Photo: Robert Owen)

Four
Around Egremont

Mother Redcap's, photographed in July 1958, was originally a private residence in 1595 but became an inn in 1770, with Polly Jones as its landlady who wore a red cap. She hid seamen from the press gangs and was trusted with their valuables. There were supposed to be underground passages and caves where smuggled goods were hidden. The building was pulled down in 1974 and a nursing home is now in its place. (Photo: Medley)

Crowds walk along the extended promenade in the 1930s. Children play on the steps and rails. People, both heavily and modestly clad, enjoy the sands. The Town Hall, built between 1914 and 1920, dominates the scene. The foundation stone had been laid in 1914. When the war came it was used as a military hospital and not reused as a Town Hall until 3 November 1920.

HRH Princess Anne visits Wallasey Town Hall for a Civic Lunch on 5 July 1978. She is accompanied by Cllr. Bill Wells, who had been a Labour Party representative for the Moreton ward. (Photo: Ron Smith)

Eric Morecambe and Ernie Wise, the unforgettable comedy team, were at the Wallasey Town Hall in 1962. Eric autographed the cheek of singer, David Whitfield, watched by the Mayor and Mayoress of Wallasey, Ald. and Mrs Evan G. Roberts. (Photo: Ron Smith)

In April 1962 thirty two members receive Long Service Medals for their time in the Civil Defence and Auxiliary Fire Service. They include: J. Jones, A. Beed, R. Edwards, A. Williamson, W. White, Marion Mann, H.J. Knox, Olive Hardcastle, W.Graham, Emily Bird, J. Cox, J. Bohs, Frances Howard, T. Avery, H. Pusey, O. Bond, H. Ashworth, J.H. Jones, C. Waring, Lois Shacklady, R. Jones, A. Williams, D. Walker, P. Cross, H. Mercer, Vera Thomson, Florence Askam, Margaret Tonks, F. Mathieson, T. Taylor, E. Haws, W. Bartlett and the Mayor of Wallasey, Ald. C.G.E. Dingle. (Photo: Medley)

The *Daffodil*, a fortified Wallasey Ferry steamer, was photographed by Joe Mumford, who had studios in the Wallasey area from 1906-1938. The *Daffodil* and another ferry steamer, *Iris*, helped in the commando attack on Zeebrugge on 22 and 23 April 1918. The boats afterwards received the accolade of Royal *Iris* and Royal *Daffodil* from HM King George V.

HM the Queen and the Duke of Edinburgh aboard the *Royal Iris* on 21 June 1977. It was an appropriate vessel for the Royal Review of Mersey shipping. (Photo: Ron Smith)

This is Egremont Ferry in the 1890s. John Askew, the Liverpool Harbour Master, came from Egremont, Cumbria. He built an estate between what is now Sandon Road and Maddock Road, which he named after his native town and, with John Tobin of Liscard Hall, established a ferry in 1835. It was bought by the local board and reconstructed in 1876 as an iron pier 280 feet long.

It was only a short walk from ferry boat to promenade and sand at Egremont in the 1910s. The size of the crowd and the presence of flags and bunting suggest a special occasion, perhaps a royal visit for the laying of the Town Hall foundation stone in 1914. The first section of the promenade had been built from Seacombe Ferry to Sandon Road and then to Holland Road in 1891. Previously some of the houses stretched to the shore and had retaining walls on the embankment.

In February 1895 the River Mersey froze over as it had done in 1854-5 and in 1878. On one of these occasions Captain Alfred Godfrey of the Grebe Cock was able to walk across the Mersey from Wallasey to Liverpool, the ice was so thick.

Egremont Ferry had been damaged on a number of occasions. Its final ramming was by the coaster, *Newlands*, in 1941. As it was wartime no attempt was made to rebuild it and it was eventually dismantled in 1946.

The Wrench Series. No. 6896.

In 1905 some elderly men and women are seen here resting along the promenade below the Mariners' Home. Cliff House, with its clocktower a welcoming feature to crews and passengers passing through the Mersey, was erected in 1882 by William Cliff, a Liverpool merchant, in memory of his daughter Mrs Rosa Webster. It originally provided for 150 aged and poor British seamen.

In 1981 Cliff House, including its clocktower, was demolished as the need for a different type of accommodation emerged. The Mariners' Park estate now provides single and double linked flatlets for single and married persons, representing every category of seaman and seawoman, who are capable of continuing independent lives with the security of surveillance by resident matron and warden.

On 16 April 1907 Lord Balfour of Burleigh, a former Chief Secretary for Scotland, laid the foundation of a new Egremont Presbyterian Church at the corner of Manor Road and Seabank Road. In 1972 it became Egremont United Reformed Church when Presbyterian and Congregational churches were united.

The 'converted' old Egremont Presbyterian Church is seen here in the 1920s. It had been closed for worship in 1908, remaining empty until 1910 when it became the Lyceum Palace. The first cinema seats were the remaining church pews. A huge fire in December 1931 led to the Lyceum's demolition in 1933 and its replacement with the Gaumont Palace. It was indeed a 'palace' holding more than 1,200 patrons and with the most luxurious of furnishings and fittings. When purchased by Unit Four in 1972, the theatre became six separate cinemas.

Members of the photographic firm of Medley and Bird hold a party in the 1950s at their premises in King Street. During the 1950s and 1960s most Wallaseyans would have been photographed at school, at work or at special events by one of these photographers. Among people at the party were: Monica (reception), Eileen Medley, Bob Bird, Robin Bird (with hands over ears and now Editor, *Wirral Globe*), Rosemary, Rose Smith (mother of Ron and Noël), Nellie Walker, Tony Donavan, Lesley Bird, Stuart Fordham, Keith Medley, Ron Smith.

In Memoriam: one of the photographers was Ron Smith seen in Medley and Bird's King Street studios. He is standing by a large format plate camera which sitters used to face when going for a portrait photograph. Professional photographers still use large format cameras in their work for the best possible quality. Ron Smith had studied photography with his friend Graham Stark, a well-known Wallasey born actor and himself an accomplished professional studio photographer.

Even in 1950 professional press photographers, like Keith Medley here, still used large plate cameras which could block out the view and ruin many a good photograph. Wallasey's social history of the 1950s and 1960s is encapsulated in thousands of Medley negatives recorded on glass plates. Keith Medley has also worked as a ciné photographer for the major television companies.

On 30 June 1994 Bob Bird, photographed by his son Frazer, was honoured by the *Daily Post* as Merseyside's oldest working photographer at 73 years of age. He is still working and regularly has his photographs published in Liverpool and Wirral newspapers. In the course of his work, he has accumulated 20,000 negatives and 2,000 news films.

This house, 1, Falkland Street, photographed about 1980, was formerly the studios of Priestley and Son, professional photographers. This studio was in active use from 1896 to 1938, although members of the Priestley family had studios in Buchanan Street, Seacombe, Walmsley Street North, Egremont, and also in Claughton and Oxton. The side building was used for processing plates, films and prints.

This photograph, taken between 1915 and 1918, of Wallasey Red Cross VAD was photographed by Priestley and Son and printed at 1, Falkland Street. During the First World War the partially completed Wallasey Town Hall, the Children's Hospital Leasowe, opened in 1914, and other public buildings were used to treat the wounded servicemen.

This photograph of Serpentine Road, Egremont, was taken at 'the top end' by Martin's Lane in about 1904. The photographer was Arthur Shaw of 32, Briardale Road, Seacombe, who had a studio there from 1901-9. He also had a studio in Brighton Street from 1909 to 1920.

Miss Moore is seen in the garden of her parents' home in the 1920s. Her father had a carriage and stables. Miss Moore had been a pupil at Seabank School and later became Mrs Earley.

Five

Around Liscard

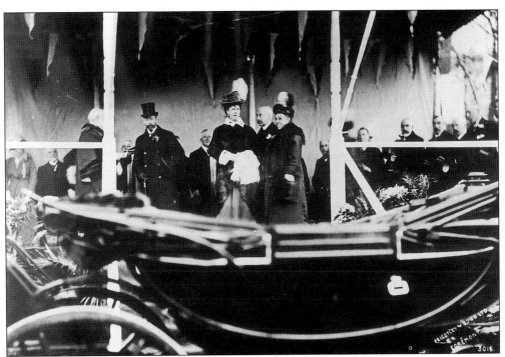

On 25 March 1914 HM King George V, accompanied by HM Queen Mary, pressed a lever in Central Park and 'let loose' an electric current that laid the foundation for the Town Hall at North Meade, Brighton Street, Seacombe. As usual Priestley and Sons were there to record the event for posterity.

In 1911, on the occasion of the Coronation of HM King George V and Queen Mary, Wallasey celebrated with a festival in Central Park. The band of the Navy League Seatraining Home took part in many Wallasey events and can be seen near the bandstand.

Swan Pond
and School of Art,
Central Park, Liscard.

In about 1910 a family look at the inhabitants of the Swan Pond. In the background is the former School of Art which was once Liscard Hall. Sir John Tobin, a Manxman, who had built his fortune in the slave trade, became Mayor of Liverpool in 1819 and built Liscard Hall in the early 1830s. His son-in-law, Harold Littledale, a Liverpool merchant, followed as the owner and when he died in 1889, the Hall was purchased by the Wallasey Board for art students who were formerly taught at the Concert Hall in Manor Road.

A number of cricket teams have played in Central Park. Mr B. Dobson believes that he may be the only one to have played for three of them. In the 1950s he played for the Egremont CC and recalled that their pavilion burnt down. He later played for Liscard CC which celebrated its centenary in 1992. Its tea room/dressing room was destroyed by vandals in 1972 but it was restored by the club who went on to enjoy a very productive period. Here is the 1973 Liscard CC team: G. Hughes, E. Whitby, M. Deegan, T. Meadows, S. Jones, J. Taylor, N. Sandiford, B. Dobson, D. Fleming, K. Williams, C. Jones.

Mr B. Dobson also played for Park Field CC at Central Park. Park Field CC had begun its cricket life as St John's CC. Here is the 1975 team: J. Long, A. Brooke, J. Williams, A. Costain, B. Davies, B. Kenyon, D. O'Connell, P. Stevenson, E. Eccles, B. Dobson, D. Robson.

In about 1910 the Concert Hall, right foreground, in Liscard Road, with its large verandah, where ladies would wait for their carriages, has been used for many purposes. Wallasey High School for girls was founded in the Concert Hall in 1883 under its first Head, Miss Eaton, and remained there until 1890. The school had several moves before settling in Mount Pleasant. In the foreground left, the Old Court House was used for Wallasey's police force until, in 1914, the building became a cinema. From 1949 the cinema showed mainly continental films and it remained as 'The Continental', serving coffee during the interval, until 1963.

In about 1890 a policeman and a postman are seen walking along Liscard Road near Walsingham Road. Before 1913 they belonged to the North Wirral Division of the Cheshire County Constabulary. At midnight on 31 March 1913 the Wallasey Police Force of ninety men was formed. In the background on the right is the Presbyterian Church.

Taken in Mill Lane about 1910 this photograph shows two landmarks of Liscard, the Water Tower and St Albans Church. The cottages on the left were designed for workers on Littledale's Model Farm. Among the innovations that Littledale introduced were ventilated shippons for the cattle and a multipurpose steam engine that not only ground the corn but also churned the milk to make butter.

In about 1904 St Alban's Roman Catholic Church had been standing for sixty-two years. Catholic worship in Wallasey had begun in an inn in Seacombe called The Hen and Chickens. A poll in the 1960s placed St Albans among the buildings Wallaseyans would most like to see preserved. Keenan's cottage on the opposite side of the road, became Granny Smith's cottage where the key to the fire engine was kept. The horses were obtained from Gibbon's stable yard which was where the Capitol building is today.

Liscard AFC in 1918 was one of the many amateur teams playing in the Wallasey area. They were photographed here by 'Wilkinson'. It was probably the photographer James Wilkinson who had a studio in Manville Road, New Brighton, from 1912 to 1938. The other Wilkinsons, Marmaduke, Martha and William, operated in their respective studios in the Lower Parade, New Brighton, during the latter years of the nineteenth century.

Among the players in this 1951 Liscard School Intermediate Team are: Cyril Rylett, Billy McLachlan, Gordon Cowie, Brian Edge, Barrie Dennis, Stan Billington, David Stroud, Ronnie Carson. Barrie Dennis (centre, back row) and Stan Billington (centre, front, holding the ball) played for Cheshire. Billington later played for England Schoolboys.

In 1935 young members of the Marlowe Road Dance School performed on the stage of the church hall of Marlowe Road Congregational (now United Reformed) Church which at that time was only eight years old.

Perhaps the youngsters above had ambitions to become members of the prestigious Wallasey Operatic Society. Here are members rehearsing for a 1962 production of *Kiss Me Kate* to be performed at the Royal Court Theatre, Liverpool. Among the members of the cast were: L. Campbell and R. Muir (principals), P. French, N. Hayes, F. Jalland, M. Munro, C. Berwick, R. Goudie, M. Daniel, R. Bartram, P. Walker and D. Kelly. Musical Director was H. Uren and choreographer, H. Hylton Bromley.

By about 1918, Liscard village shops had again taken over as the fashionable area for ladies who came by carriage to shop. The building to the left, The Monkey House, is still mentioned with affection as a gathering place. The gentlemen's toilet situated down steps beneath is still recalled by residents who search in vain for such facilities today. The horse and cart is standing by Williams Bros. Grocers where Mr York was manager in 1912 before moving to his own shop in Wallasey Village.

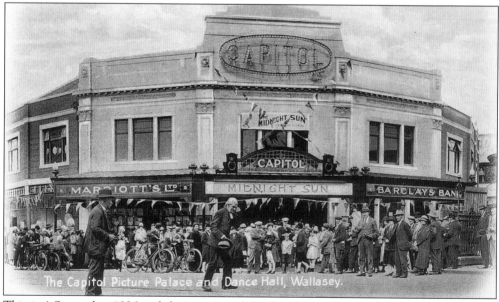

This is 4 September 1926 and the opening of the Capitol cinema on the site of Gibbons the undertaker who had kept horses and carriages there. The main actors in this presentation at the opening were Pat O' Malley and Laura La Plante, who was to star as Magnolia in the 1929 film *Showboat*. A.E. Davey, a local artist, painted the titles and illustrations for the forthcoming week as soon as the previous week's showing ended.

74

In 1964 the island at the crossroads was prepared and ready for planting to make a colourful display. Two buses are seen. A cream Wallasey No. 10 bus is on its way to New Brighton and a blue Birkenhead No. 10 bus on its way to the New Ferry depot. (Photo: Medley)

This scene is from about 1980. The flowers have gone and the cinema closed its doors on 23 February 1974. The stars of its final double bill were respectively, Cliff Richard and Jack Palance. The Capitol reopened as a Bingo Hall in 1978. (Photo: Medley)

In 1937 the old and the new Wellington Hotels stand together. When the new one was completed the old one was demolished.

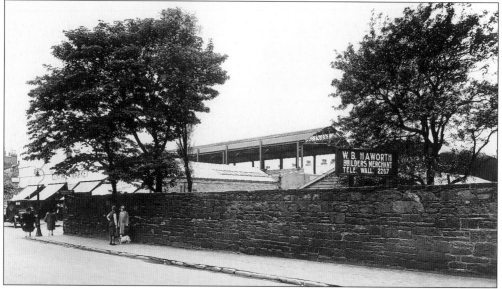

At the same time, in 1937, this area in Wallasey Road was being developed. The Central Market, with its stalls offering meat, fruit, vegetables, fancy goods and secondhand books, was being dismantled to construct Coronation Buildings. One of the new shops was Strothers which in 1962 was advertising a 17 inch TV set for £25. Builders' merchant William Blackburn Haworth who had to move had begun his business in Poulton near the Penny Bridge.

In 1995 Oldershaw School celebrated the 75th Anniversary of its opening on 11 September 1920. This was the first photograph of a team taken in the school. This intermediate football team took on the rest of the school and was all conquering. Top row: Thorpe, MadocJones (first headboy), Bostock, Beatty, Anderson. Middle row: Paget, McWilliam, Cockburn, Jones, Thorsen. Front: Seymour, Helm.

Here is the Oldershaw cricket team of 1944-45. Back row: Gerrard Senior, Irving, Beardsell, Kenny, O' Brien, Gaynor. Front row: Howard, Smith, Young, Wilson, Peers, Dyson.

In the season 1962-63 this was the Oldershaw 1st XV Rugby team. Left to right, back row: Crook, de Boer, Newins, MacAulay, Tattum, Purland, Roberts, McTeer, Fielding. Front row: Foster, Turner, Burgess, Kennedy (Capt.), Fisher, Chrystal, Birkett, Johnson.

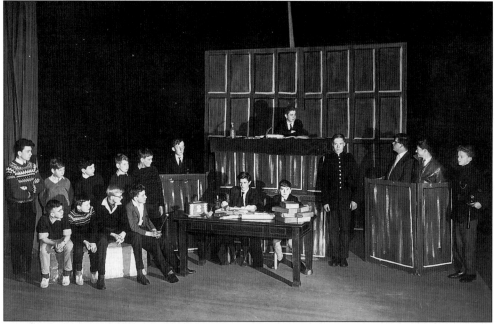

In 1963 boys in Oldershaw School performed *Emil and the Detectives*. The school has had a strong tradition in dramatic productions which have included *The Rivals* (1953) and *King Lear* (1958). Oldershaw Girls' School took its productions abroad, including *Tobias and the Angel* and *Romeo and Juliet*. Since Oldershaw School's mixed comprehensive status, *Grease* (1990) and *Guys and Dolls* (1991) have been added to the repertoire.

In June 1965 the captain of Oldershaw School's Road Safety Cycle team was presented with a Borough trophy by the Mayor Cecil Tomkins and Mrs Tomkins. The other members of the team were: Lovell, Chadwick, T. Jones, Forsyth and Smith. (Photo: Bob Bird)

In the 1990s a class of Oldershaw School pupils learn a foreign language through a 'real-life' technique of ordering a meal in a cafe in French.

This was Hoseside Road in about 1905. The name was derived from 'hoes' meaning 'sandhills'. The scene is near the Captain's Pit. When the wife of a captain heard of his death at sea, she threw herself in and drowned and was said to haunt Liscard Castle. There was a Hoseside Farm and also an Oarside Farm whose proprietor, Mr Blackburn, advertised that his farm was available for Sunday school treats and other parties to have swings, donkey rides and other entertainment, with catering in a pavilion amidst 'tall and umbrageous trees'.

Although the sign over the shop in Mount Pleasant declared that F. Challoner was a cycle expert, a 1926 guide gave his profession as motor engineer. He may also have owned the Service Automobile Co. which was next door.

Wallasey School, which celebrated its 400th anniversary in 1995, occupied these premises from 1876 to 1911. This photograph was taken in 1910. A school prospectus at the time specified unequivocally that 'no boy is admitted to the school except on condition of conformity to rules laid down by the authorities'.

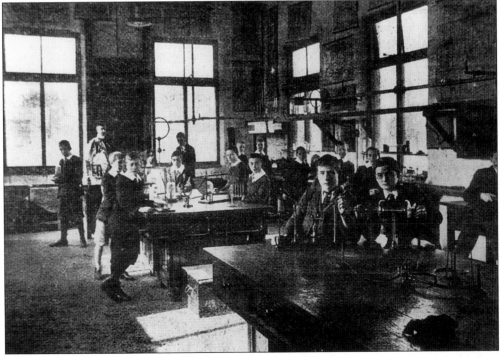

This was the physics laboratory of Wallasey School in 1910.

Not only was Wallasey School successful academically but also excelled at games and sports. Neil McKechnie, seen here with commentator Kenneth Wolstenholme, was an international swimmer whilst still at school. By 1956 he held five British swimming records of the Amateur Swimming Association. Wallasey's provision of swimming baths was a factor in his success and that of Lilian Preece an international swimmer from 1949 to 1954. More than 250 National, European and World Championship Records have been broken at Guinea Gap Baths.

In September 1962, a team of Wallasey School old boys, The Old Wallaseyans Seven, won the Sunday Times Cup at the Old Haberdashers' Club, Boreham Wood, Hertfordshire. The successful team was, left to right: P. Townsend, A. Flood (Capt.), D. Bowers, D. Hackett, R. Brunskill, P. Treganza, D. Stanford.

There was a youthful military presence in Wallasey. Clifton Hall which adjoined Wallasey School in Withens Lane was transposed into the Navy League's Sea Training Home in 1897 to become the first land sea school in the country. The school's band took part in many civic functions. The school continued until it was evacuated during the Second World War. Its building was taken over in 1949 as the Wallasey Technical College.

On 5 May 1962 Army Cadets gathered in their headquarters off Seabank Road to admire the trophy won by their Commanding Officer, Lt. D.A.W. Noakes. Later Lt. Noakes became the Commandant of the Cheshire Army Cadet Force.

Seabank High School, seen here about 1905 in Seabank Road, was opened in 1892 and known as Miss Earp's Ladies' School. It later moved to 'King's Court' in Penkett Road and offered a wide curriculum including gymnastics, art, swimming and commercial subjects. It closed in 1940. Brothers of the girls often chose to go to Liscard High School, also known as Wrigley's.

Former members of Seabank High School formed an association with the purpose of rendering service to the community. Members met (and still meet) in each other's houses to raise money for charitable objects. On 12 August 1967 Old Seabankians took local handicapped children to Llandudno for the day.

In summer 1963 children from Westbourne School, Penkett Road, performed a play based on the story of the *Pied Piper of Hamelin*. Westbourne School was founded in 1948 for children aged four to eleven and taken over by its present owner Mr T.N. Cottam in 1953. (Photo: Medley)

In 1966 Westbourne School pupils took part in the play of *Aladdin*. Mrs Jean Jenkins, who taught the kindergarten class, had a son, Martin, at the school. He became a director of Radio Drama at the BBC. (Photo: Medley)

Children of Marymount Convent School in 1946.

This was the final match of the season for New Brighton AFC (The Rakers) at Sandheys Park on 2 May 1925. In 1898 a New Brighton team joined the Football League and in the first season finished on equal points, 5th, with Newton Heath, now Manchester United. The first New Brighton team functioned until 1901 but this New Brighton AFC was formed in 1921. Team, left to right, back row: Carney, Niven, Heyes (asst. trainer), Reid, Critchlow, Watson (trainer), Davies, Jones, Hird, Lacey, Spencer, Leadbetter, Gutteridge. Seated: Gemmell, Whitter, Wade, Wilcox, J. Jones, Mehaffy, Mathieson, Gee, Denwood. Front: Kelly, J. Reid, Gaffney, Walker, Waine.

New Brighton AFC was not re-elected in 1951 after finishing bottom of the Third Division North. In this cup tie with Stockport County, Johnny Vincent of New Brighton saw his header saved by the opposing goalkeeper. Long serving trainer Ernie Longden lives in Wallasey and is keenly interested in local history. (Photo: R. Smith)

Six

Around The Waterfront

Harrison Drive To The Ham And Egg Parade

The 'Residents' Pool', Derby Baths, was opened at Harrison Drive in 1937 by Lord Derby. It complemented the Bathing Station which had been built in 1927. The bath was 330ft long 75ft wide and could accommodate 850 in the water and 1,000 spectators looking on. There were balconies for 200 sun bathers. The pool was demolished in 1984.

In about 1920 carefully dressed men and women stroll along the embankment at 'Harrison Drive'. Clothes for the office and clothes for the seaside were barely distinguishable. The area from Grove Road station down to the front was always called Harrison Drive. It was named after James Harrison, founder of the Harrison Shipping Line, who gave Harrison Park to the public in memory of his parents. Before the Second World War, tents were brought to this part of the shore. A bathing station and a café were erected nearby in 1927.

In 1947 this section of Harrison Drive was particularly popular with residents and with those who did not want to mix their seaside relaxation with amusement parks and shops. The Welsh hills are clearly visible from here. (Photo: Oxton Studios: 01516528690)

In 1936 people gathered by the model boating pool to sail or watch model yachts. The waters had previously lapped the Red Noses where there was once a Noah's Ark café in a wrecked boat. In 1939 the promenade from Seacombe to Harrison Drive was finally completed. The Red Noses are now inland behind railings.

Fifty years later in 1986, children are more casually dressed and the boats on the pool are now more likely to be radio controlled than wind driven, especially when fathers and grandfathers take over in the evening. On the skyline the dome of SS Peter's and Paul's church is clearly visible. The church on top of St George's Mount, built in 1932, has a copper covered dome with a span of eighty-six feet and is known to mariners as The Dome of Home.

91

In 1983 the title of Miss New Brighton was won by Vicki Ellis of Little Sutton. In 1960 Joan Boardman was the first winner from Wallasey and in 1977 it was won by Tracey Nielson Steele of Moreton. The popular contest was held annually between 1949 and 1989. (Photo: Ron Smith)

Photographer Keith Medley seems to be enjoying his work as he escorts two of the finalists in the Miss New Brighton contest in the 1950s to be photographed. (Photo: Medley)

At the final in 1950 not everyone, apparently was interested in the beauty contest. No doubt the young bored spectator would have preferred to swim in the pool which had been opened on 13 June 1934. It was one of the largest in the world and could accommodate 4,000 bathers and 20,000 spectators. Hurricane force gales in 1990 brought about its demolition. (Photo: Medley)

It is 1948 and the holiday crowds are still attracted to New Brighton in their thousands. There are few cars about and a bus stop by Victoria Gardens indicates that buses to Arrowe Park are available. Most buses at this time went from Virginia Road at the back of the Floral Pavilion. For many day trippers from Liverpool, the ferry boat ride from New Brighton pier was the only proper way to end the day. (Photo: Oxton Studios: 01516528690)

There have been many types of amusements and rides in Kings Parade between the baths and the Marine Lake. This was a 1986 version.

In 1986 there was also a Peter Pan railway opposite Marine Gardens.

Bank Holiday at New Brighton

In about 1900 there was a lot of sand around the Perch Rock area between tides before the Marine Lake was constructed. It is possible to date this postcard as before 1902. It was only permissible to write the address on the back and messages had to be written around the picture. In 1902 the British postal services permitted a line to be drawn on the back to allow the message to be written on the left of the line and the address to be written on the right.

On 31 May 1933 the people are waiting in their deckchairs for Ald. Walter Eastwood to formally declare the Marine Lake open for boat rides, canoeing and rowing. The ten acres site had cost £95,000 to build. After the storms of 1990 the lake has been mainly used by canoeists and by a school for training yachtsmen. (Photo: Medley)

In about 1904 tall sailing ships were still seen in the Mersey. Peter Bourne, Mayor of Liverpool, laid the first stone of the Battery on Fort Perch Rock on 31 March 1826. Originally it had thirty-two pounder guns to protect shipping but in the Second World War there were two 6 inch guns. Ships paid a sixpenny levy as they passed through the Mersey to help maintain it. By 1976 the Battery had become derelict until architect, Norman Kingham, spent £250,000 on its restoration. In 1996 it was again put up for sale. The lighthouse nearby was inaugurated on 1 March 1830 replacing wooden structures. The new lighthouse was constructed of granite and coated with a hardening volcanic material from Mount Etna. Norman and Cassandra Kingham also had the lighthouse restored and it has been used as an unusual venue for weekend breaks and honeymoons.

In 1960 there were still large crowds of holidaymakers on the promenade, by Fort Perch Rock and on the New Brighton shore. (Photo: Medley)

In about 1915 these riders on the donkeys have reached the limit of the ride which went to Wallasey shore from New Brighton and back. There is a sign in the background indicating the way to Wallasey station. There was also a station at Warren, especially for golfers, but this closed on 1 October 1916. This section of the line used to get covered with sand and an embarrassing £2,000 was spent annually to clear it.

By 1950 Jack Clarke had been a popular donkeyman for twenty years. Members of the Clarke family, who mostly lived in Egerton Street, were closely associated with horses and donkeys over several generations. Bob Clarke, for example, kept horses for hire at stables in Alexandra Road. Riders would take them along the shore as far as Leasowe and back. Lily Clarke married Bert Felton and they took photographs of visitors in the Tower grounds. (Photo: Medley)

Wind speeds of up to 100 mph have been recorded in New Brighton. The waves crashing around Fort Perch Rock indicate the force with which vessels have to contend at times. On 3 December 1909 the Isle of Man mailboat, *Ellan Vannin*, launched as *Isle the Second* in 1860, lost all of its twenty-one crew and fifteen passengers off New Brighton in a Force 12 gale.

On 24 January 1863 this tubular lifeboat was launched to serve at the New Brighton station. Between 60,000 and 70,000 people turned out as it was paraded around the town. The event was recorded in the *Illustrated London News* of 7 February 1863. Over 1,000 lives have been saved by the New Brighton lifeboat crews since 1863.

On 19 August 1920 the Isle of Man steamer, *King Orry III*, ran aground near New Brighton lighthouse. Local firemen took the passengers off the ship. The *King Orry III* had been launched at Cammell Laird's in Birkenhead on 11 March 1913. It went to help in the evacuation of Dunkirk but it was bombed and destroyed on 29 March 1940.

This is the New Brighton lifeboat landing in 1961 after its crew had made a rescue. The ferry boat *Wallasey* is in the background. (Photo: Medley)

This is the *Norman B. Corlett* lifeboat, in service from 1950 to 1973, before the wheelhouse was fitted in 1963. The naming ceremony was attended by HRH Duchess of Kent in Princes Dock, Liverpool. The lifeboat was donated by the parents of Norman Corlett who lost his life in a yachting accident. The ship is still afloat in Crosshaven, Ireland. (Information: P. and J. Hockey)

This is an aerial view of New Brighton in the 1950s from the Palace to the Seacombe Ferry. New Brighton still had its pier, its Tower pleasure grounds and football ground.

This panoramic view in the early 1900s shows the Tower, erected 1896-1908 and fifty feet higher than Blackpool Tower, the Ham and Egg Parade, the Palace and the Pavilion. The Palace set out to be an amusement centre that catered for every need and included salt water baths, an aviary, ballroom dancing, a skating rink, classical music and the new animated pictures.

Members of the Wilkie family have had close associations with the Palace and the Pavilion for generations. Here is one of their amusements from the early 1900s.

Wilmer Wilkie ran a circus from the 1940s in the area where the Pavilion used to be. Here it is in the 1950 season. Seats were 1/6 to 6/- (7p to 30p). When Wilmer Wilkie took the circus to South Africa, his son, Bill Wilkie, took over the management of the Palace. (Photo: Oxton Studios: 01516528690)

Elephants parade along Atherton Street to publicise Wilkie's Circus in about 1950. (Photo: Medley)

On a wet Sunday afternoon in 1978 day trippers still find interest in looking at the ships passing by.

In 1978 on that same wet day this child was enjoying a ride in the Palace indoor fair.

In this 1890s photograph of the Upper Terrace or Aquarium Parade the intended gentility of the New Brighton resort is apparent.

By 1905 the parade had become brash and vulgar with 'teapot' shops below and cheap boarding houses in the terrace above. There were shooting galleries and makeshift photographic studios on the beach. Fortune tellers, street hawkers, pickpockets, fighting and 'goings on' in the area earned it the derogatory title of the 'Ham and Egg Parade'.

In 1905 the 'Ham and Egg Parade' was acquired by the local council and converted into the Victoria Gardens and the Floral Pavilion Theatre. It is seen here in about 1936 when *Pleasure on Parade* was the current show.

In 1950 the Melody Inn revue had been running for two years and it continued until 1970 under the direction of Jackson Earle and his wife, Peggy Naylor. The Floral Pavilion was also the venue for amateur productions like the Chrysanthemums 'Spectacular' Pantomimes and one night appearance by artistes like Cilla Black, Petula Clark, Tommy Handley, Robb Wilton, Wilfred Pickles, Cavan O'Connor, Val Doonican and Harry Seacombe.

This was the Floral Pavilion in 1932. At first shows had been given in the open air from 1913 but in 1925 it was roofed over with glass. In 1938 under the direction of Frank Terry and company, the BBC regularly broadcast shows of the New Brighton Follies.

Jackson Earle is seen here in the 1960s receiving kisses from two contestants in a heat of Miss New Brighton which he was judging. The *Melody Inn* revue, which he produced, played before 80,000 patrons a year. Its appeal came from his sincerity and that of his regular cast of Peggy Naylor and Mavis White (*The Two Judies*), Jimmy Mac, Joe Ring and other favourites. At Jackson Earle's funeral in January 1971 at St James' Church, New Brighton, more than 600 people crowded into the church, including the Mayor and other civic dignitaries. The minister said of him that he cared about people and gave them of his best. (Photo: R. Smith)

Seven
Around Victoria Road and the Pier

In July 1981 members of the staff of Forber and Sons, grocers, of Victoria Road, celebrated the royal wedding in style and provided a happy welcome to New Brighton. (Photo: R. Bird)

This was the scene that day trippers and holidaymakers would encounter when they reached New Brighton in about 1910. Most notable would be the twin landmarks of St James's Church and the 621 feet Tower. As passengers entered the station offices they would be reminded that Beaty Brothers could provide tailoring in Wallasey and, in Liverpool, pianos were available from Van Cruisen and watches from Russell's.

In 1886 the Mersey Railway tunnel was opened and in 1888 the line was extended to New Brighton. Atherton had planned that New Brighton should accommodate the gentry. The gentlefolk are in evidence here in about 1910. The gentleman in the foreground is facing away from the station and looking towards the Seacombe line. Above him on the left is the Hotel Victoria which is still a landmark and revered hostelry today. In 1923 it was possible to travel to London from New Brighton via West Kirby and Hooton. The line from Liverpool was electrified on 13 March 1938.

Cafés abounded in Victoria Road. Many were 'snug, warm, beautifully decorated' and could claim that all meals served were 'all fresh food'. Others catered for more basic tastes as this advertisement for the Rialto Café in 1933 shows. For those who wished to stay for a holiday in New Brighton there were plenty of hotels and guest houses. In 1933 it would cost only £2 2s 0d (£2 10p) per week for full board at a comfortable guest house near the sea front

In about 1905 this Convalescent Home, which had been built in Wellington Road in 1847, was for women. They were allowed to bring their children with them. In 1924 the Sisters of the Holy Family of Bordeaux converted the home into a girls' school called Maris Stella. At one time there were 500 girls in the school. When St Mary's College was built in Wallasey Village in 1972, Maris Stella School closed. The site is now home to a block of flats and sheltered accommodation.

Maris Stella School in 1953.

In about 1904 Victoria Road was a quality street as witnessed by the clothes worn by the ladies and by the presence of Webster's bookshop on the right.

This scene in Victoria Road in about 1935 again emphasises the quality of the road. The people in the picture are formally dressed. Many visitors came to New Brighton just for shopping in Victoria Road which was at least as enjoyable as sitting on the sands. Among the shops visible on the right are Boots the Cash Chemists, P. Flinn, chiropodist, and the Camera Shop. Victoria Road was noted for its high class ladies' fashion shops, chinaware, shoe shops and music stores.

In 1935 Robin Jones (manager), Miss Walsh (cashier), and other members of the staff of the Trocadero stand in front of the cinema as publicity to advertise that a film of the Grand National would be shown as well as the main feature *The Man Who Knew Too Much*, which starred Leslie Banks, an actor from Wirral. The Trocadero had been opened by the Mayor, Ald. A. Quinn, on 1 June 1922. It was a grand cinema with a symphony orchestra, a typical Wallasey feature, and could be contrasted with the neighbouring 'Court's' cosiness. (Photo: Clive Garner)

The Trocadero closed on 22 May 1956. This photograph was taken in April 1983. The LoCost supermarket operated for a time from the premises. Only the 'CAD' part of the original TROCADERO sign was visible. Now the building has been demolished.

In 1905 an open-topped tram is turning at the 'horseshoe' by the pier. In 1879 horse-drawn trams were introduced to run between Field Road (off Rowson Street) and Seacombe via Rake Lane and Liscard Village. Electric trams took over in 1902. Large letters and coloured lights were later used to indicate routes: S (dark blue) Seabank Road, RL (Amber) Rake Lane, WD (White) Warren Drive, P (Green) Poulton. Sometimes coloured flags flew from the trolley ropes of the trams whenever ferry boats were unable to operate. Blue meant no boat from New Brighton and red, no boat from Egremont.

By 1917 four tramway lines had replaced the horseshoe which caused delays when trams had to wait in a queue. As this was a First World War postcard it had to be passed by the Press Bureau for publication. In 1920 motor buses were introduced to supplement the trams which ceased to run in 1933.

This audience in about 1932 is enjoying a follies type show on the recently restructured pier (1931). There was also a high class café, bar and lounge with 'beautifully attired waitresses'.

This group of Pierrots, about 1908, was called the Royal Mascots. Adeler and Sutton's Pierrots were successful performers on the pier at the end of the nineteenth century. Pierrots generally were a feature of shows on New Brighton pier, parks and the sands. They appeared in the Pavilion on the pier until it was closed in 1923. Various concert parties and bands replaced the pierrots as attractions.

On 9 May 1973 the last passenger walkway of the pier was lifted by the Mersey Docks and Harbour Board crane, Mammoth. Gales and high seas with a 29 feet tide in 1962 had led to such damage of the bridge that the ferry service ceased. With New Brighton's future seen as more residential than tourist the demolition of the pier was seen as inevitable. (Photo: Medley)

In 1978 this was all that remained of the pier after demolition.

Eight

Around the Tower
and Vale Park

Children play on the beach. The Tower and Vale Park are in the background.

In the 1920s the Tivoli Theatre was at its height under the dynamic management of Fred (F.V.) Ross. Lily Langtry, 'The Jersey Lily', the best regarded artiste in vaudeville, was the star of this opening production. In 1928 Gaumont British acquired the theatre and put on shows and films. On reopening after the Second World War, the theatre was served by Frank Fortescue's Players and Harry Hanson's Court Players until its closure in April 1955. It was then an amusement arcade until a fire in 1976. In 1996 a block of flats was built on the site.

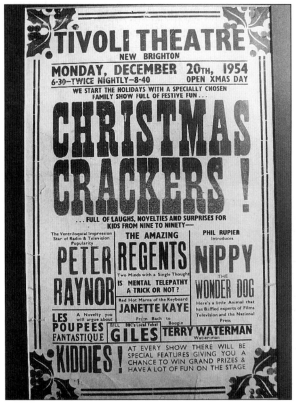

This was the programme on Monday 20 December 1954. (Michael Thomas Collection)

The ferry boat has arrived at the landing stage bringing yet more people to join the crowds on the beach by the boating pool, to visit the Tivoli Theatre or to join in the amusements in the Tower grounds. All the remembered favourite rides and sideshows may be seen in this picture, such as the Kentucky Derby, Noah's Ark, the helter skelter, the Monte Carlo Rally and the Big Dipper. Over 32 million people travelled on the ferries to Wallasey in 1919-20.

It is wartime in the 1940s and a barrage balloon is over the Mersey. The Octopus takes centre stage, behind it are the dodgem cars and to the right is the famous New Brighton 'Wall of Death' where motor cycle riders rode horizontally around the wall at breakneck speed.

In 1902 pleasures were taken at a more leisurely pace on a gondola in the lake in the Tower grounds. The photographer Henri Kostrovitzki had a studio at 100, Brighton Street, Seacombe, in 1902.

In 1948 speed was the requirement with motor boats on the lake and racing cars on the speedway. (Photo: Oxton Studios: 01516528690)

Inside the highest Tower in the country was also the largest ballroom in Europe with the finest parquetry sprung floor. It was just one of the many attractions among the 30 acres of beautiful gardens lit by 30,000 lights. For example in 1904, it was possible to enjoy animated pictures by the Royal Biograph of the Russo-Japanese War, a Himalayan Railway, a water chute, grand variety twice a day, a menagerie, a classical orchestra conducted by Charles Reynolds and Wild West shows, with real cowboys and Indians. Modern theme parks pale by comparison!

On 3 January 1911 the first Mayoral Ball was held in the ballroom for the Mayor, James Thomas Chester, civic dignitaries and other guests. On 14 June 1963 The Beatles and Gerry and the Pacemakers performed there.

In 1944 Bert Yates and the Rhythmics were performing in the Tower Ballroom as the resident band. Sometimes Bill Gregson and his band took over and most of the best known bands of the day guested there, including Joe Loss and Victor Sylvester. The Eddie Mendoza Seven and Harry Gold and his Pieces of Eight performed on the pier.

In 1945 a Civil Defence concert was held in the Tower Theatre for Victory Celebrations. A presentation was made to Ian Fraser, Wallasey's 'Frogman' VC. In February 1941 the Home Secretary, Herbert Morrison, paid a personal visit to congratulate the Civil Defence Services of Wallasey for setting an example to the rest of the country. During the war 324 local people were killed, including 174 in one night and 30 people in one shelter. A total of 658 High Explosive bombs fell on Wallasey destroying 1,150 houses and damaging 17,000 others.

The Tower had been neglected during the First World War and had become a dangerous structure. It was demolished between 7 May 1919 and June 1921. More than 1,000 tons of steel were taken away.

In 1969 the remaining part of the Tower buildings was destroyed by fire.

In 1951 a crowd has gathered to experience a ride on Tommy Mann's miniature railway on the sea front. The miniature train travelled around the old quarry among flowers and trees and back to the platform. Before the Second World War it was possible to hire cycles near this spot and ride them along the promenade towards Egremont Ferry and back. (Oxton Studios: 01516528690)

This postcard was sent on 17 April 1925. Postcards with a picture of the Tower were still popular even though the dismantling of the Tower had been completed in 1921. Carpet beds were a feature of Vale Park and Ald. and Mrs John Pennington, Mayor and Mayoress in 1943-45, presented a floral clock, but it is no longer a feature of the park.

In 1978 a family enjoy a free band concert in Vale Park, 'a sylvan retreat'. Only deckchair patrons paid. The domed roof bandstand had been erected in 1926. Some of the finest bands in the country played there, including Foden's Motor Works, Fairey Aviation, Besses o' th' Barn, and the Black Dyke Mills. Talent contests and children's shows were held there in the afternoons. One of the favourite entertainments was 'Joytime' which began in 1953.

In April 1978 the remains of the great spring storms could be seen on the promenade outside Vale Park. In the summer there were exhibitions of the work of local artists who hung their framed paintings on the railings of Vale Park.

St James's Church School was built in 1847 and was in Magazine Lane. One of its pupils who became famous was Hetty King. She was born in 1883 and made her first appearance on the London stage in 1897. From 1905 she adopted a role as male impersonator and topped the bill all over the world as a 'man about town' or as a soldier or sailor. Her most famous songs were *All the Nice Girls Love a Sailor* and *Piccadilly*. She was always immaculate as a performer and was still appearing on stage in her 80s. She died aged 89 on 28 September 1972.

This was New Brighton College as depicted in a painting of about 1860. The building had formerly been Liscard Hotel or the Stanley Arms, near Magazine Lane and the Liscard Battery. Its headmaster Dr Poggi was so admired by Garibaldi, the Italian patriot, that he sent his two sons, Ricciotti and Menotti, to study there. In 1864 the school was destroyed by fire.

On 24 June 1971 HM the Queen and Wallasey folk shared the enjoyment of the occasion at the opening of the Wallasey (Kingsway) Tunnel. (Photo: Ron Smith)

Wallasey's latest permanent residents stare out across the river as they look forward to the excitement of another phase in the development of Wallasey and round about. Unfortunately, the figures were damaged with a chainsaw. They now stand, restored, in the foyer of the Floral Pavilion.

Acknowledgements

David and Marion Rimmer are thanked for obtaining and sending photographs
and for hospitality on my numerous visits to Wallasey.
The following are thanked for providing materials and information:
Miss Mary Atkinson (Wallasey School), Miss H. Cromie (Old Seabankians),
Mrs R. Canning (Chaloner), Mrs K. Christiansen, Mr and Mrs S. Ellison, Mr B.A. Dobson,
Mr G.B. Dennis, Mr E. Gerry (postcard dealer), Mr D. Hooper, Mrs O.Jones, Mrs C. Keeling,
Mrs E. Latham, Capt. H. Morgan, Sister C. O' Reilly (Marymount), Mrs J. Price,
Mrs L. Shephard (Toolan), Mrs B. Sleeman (St George's), Mr M. Thomas,
Mr J.E. Vernon (Old Wallaseyans), Mr R. Weaver (Oldershaw), Mr K. Wolstenholme.

Kate Lomas, seen here with her friend Kitty Coffey, is symbolic of all those who care for Wallasey's past, present and future. She has a firm foundation in the history of Merseyside and is the proud holder of the prestigious 'Mermaid' award for services to nautical research. She is a member of the Friends of the Merseyside Maritime Museum and of the Wallasey Historical Society.